THE CRAZY WORLD OF GOLF

CARTOONS BY

Mike Scott

EXLEY
NEW YORK • WATFORD, UK

Other cartoon giftbooks in this series:
The Crazy World of Cats (Bill Stott)
The Crazy World of Football (Bill Stott)
The Crazy World of Gardening (Bill Stott)
The Crazy World of Housework (Bill Stott)
The Crazy World of Marriage (Bill Stott)
The Crazy World of Rugby (Bill Stott)
The Crazy World of Sex (Bill Stott)

First published in hardback in the USA in 1996 by Exley Giftbooks.
Published in Great Britain in 1996 by Exley Publications Ltd.

12   11   10   9   8   7   6   5   4   3

Copyright © Mike Scott, 1985

ISBN 1-85015-767-7

Printed in China.

Exley Publications Ltd, 16 Chalk Hill, Watford, Herts, WD1 4BN, United Kingdom.
Exley Giftbooks, 232 Madison Avenue, Suite 1206, NY 10016, USA.

"Oh, and I'll need some clubs —
those nice blue & gold ones will match my outfit."

It's the safest place...

Ah! you've found my ball!

Bunker Shot.

"I'm damned sure you forfeit a stroke for this!"

How to deal with the Golf Club Bore.

My God— Another U.F.O. Now do you believe me !

Out of bounds...

The .38 Iron.

I always dress to suit the game I expect from my opponent!

... the problem solved!

"Look at those idiots – fishing in this weather!"

You there— have you seen a golf ball land near here?

Divine Intervention...

Books in the "Crazy World" series

($6.99 £3.99 hardback)

The Crazy World of Cats (Bill Stott)
The Crazy World of Football (Bill Stott)
The Crazy World of Gardening (Bill Stott)
The Crazy World of Golf (Mike Scott)
The Crazy World of Housework (Bill Stott)
The Crazy World of Marriage (Bill Stott)
The Crazy World of Rugby (Bill Stott)
The Crazy World of Sex (Bill Stott)

Books in the "Fanatic's" series

($6.99 £3.99 hardback, also available in a larger
paperback format, $4.99, £2.99)

The Fanatic's Guides are perfect presents for
everyone with a hobby that has got out of hand.
Over fifty hilarious colour cartoons by Roland Fiddy.

The Fanatic's Guide to Cats
The Fanatic's Guide to Computers
The Fanatic's Guide to Dads
The Fanatic's Guide to D.I.Y.
The Fanatic's Guide to Golf
The Fanatic's Guide to Husbands
The Fanatic's Guide to Love
The Fanatic's Guide to Sex

Great Britain: Order these super books from
your local bookseller or from Exley Publications Ltd,
16 Chalk Hill, Watford, Herts WDI 4BN.
(Please send £1.30 to cover postage and packing
on 1 book, £2.60 on 2 or more books.)